HANDMADE
ABC
a manual alphabet

HANDMADE
ABC
a manual alphabet

Linda Bourke

✦ Addison Wesley

Copyright © 1981 by Linda Bourke
All Rights Reserved
Addison-Wesley Publishing Company, Inc.
Reading, Massachusetts 01867
Printed in the United States of America

`DEFGHIJK-WZ-898765432

Library of Congress Cataloging in Publication Data

Bourke, Linda.
    Handmade ABC.

    SUMMARY: The manual alphabet is introduced
through illustrations of each signed letter and of
items beginning with that letter.
        1. Sign language — Juvenile literature.
2. Alphabet — Juvenile literature.   [1. Sign
language. 2. Alphabet] I. Title.
P117.B6   419   80-27007
ISBN 0-201-00016-4
ISBN 0-201-00015-6 (pbk.)

For Joyce

You can recite the alphabet without moving your mouth and without making a sound. You can write your name without a pencil and paper. No magic. No tricks. Nothing up your sleeve.

How? By using the alphabet that's "made by hand" — in the air. Fingerspelling with the manual alphabet is a part of sign language used mostly for names and places. Each letter has its own hand shape and all 26 are a snap to make! Just position either hand near your mouth (not in front of it). And try not to bounce the letters.

Handmade ABC is for everyone, from Amy to Zeke. Each hand shape is presented in a bold, highly textured illustration which also shows one or more visual hints beginning with the same letter. So spell a message in the air and try your hand at guessing all the clues. Don't be surprised to find that *your* hands have quite a bit to say.

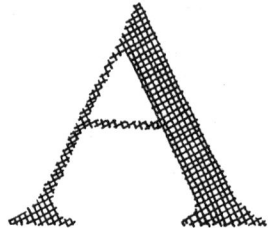

B

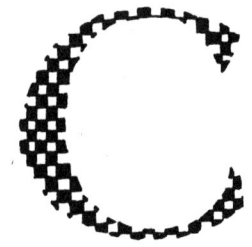

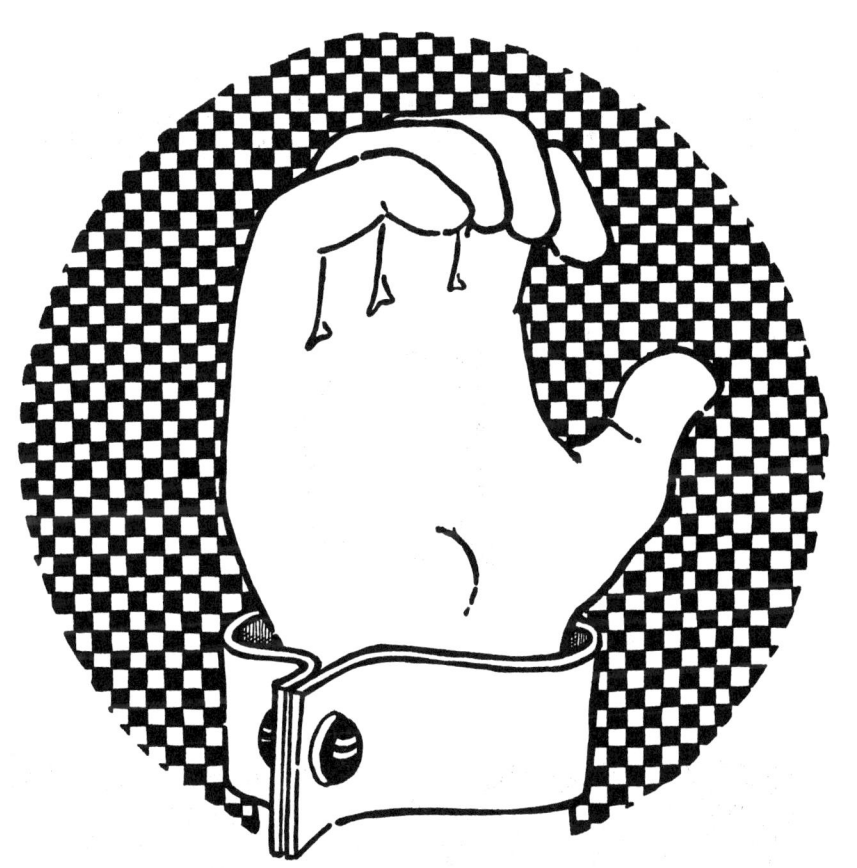

D

E

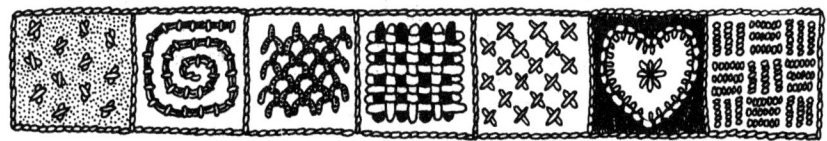

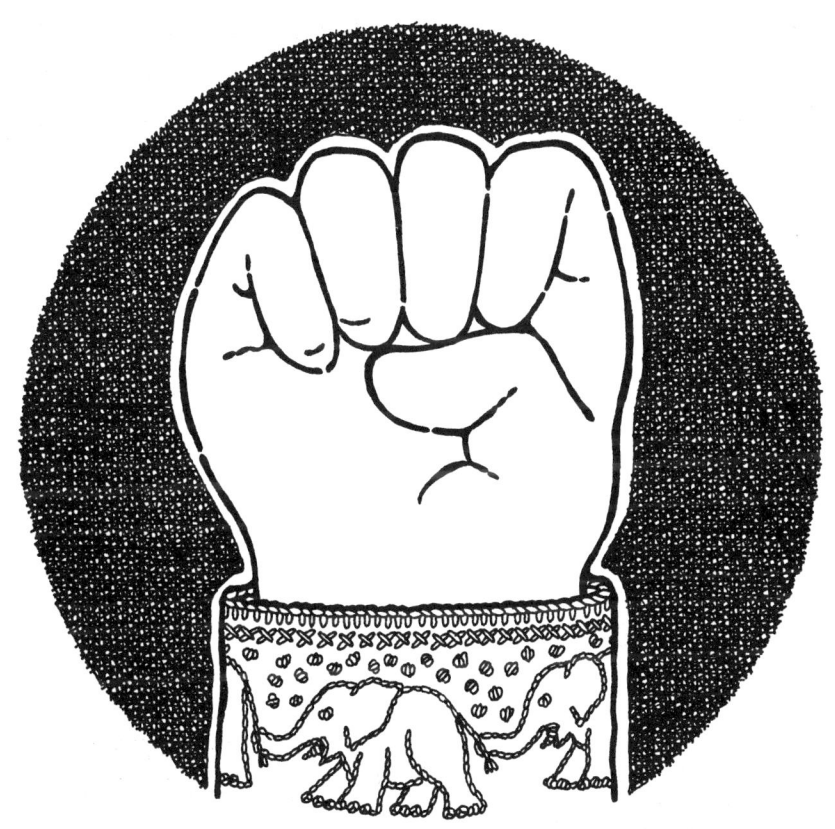

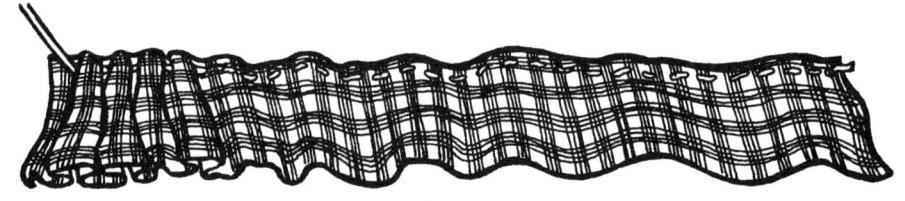

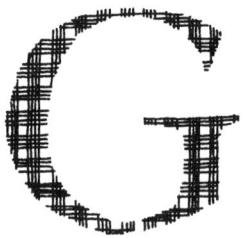

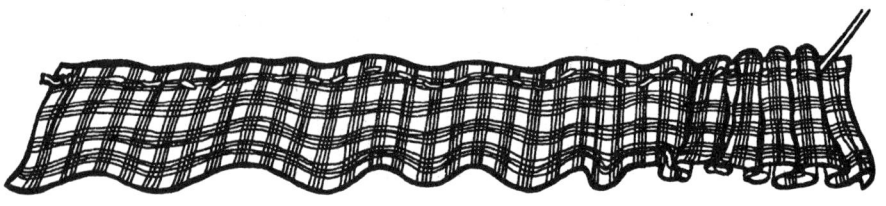

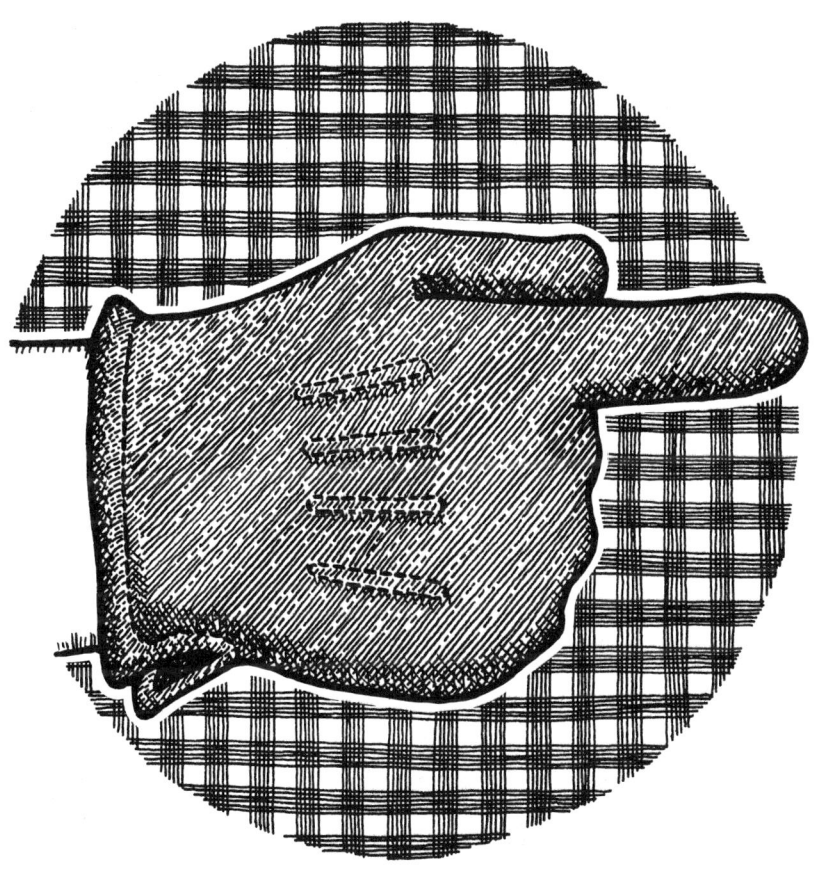

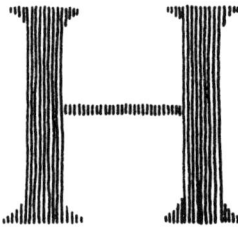

I

J

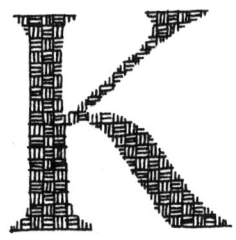

M

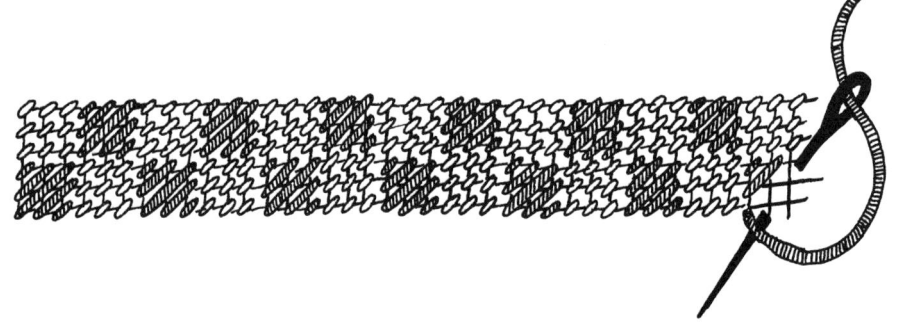

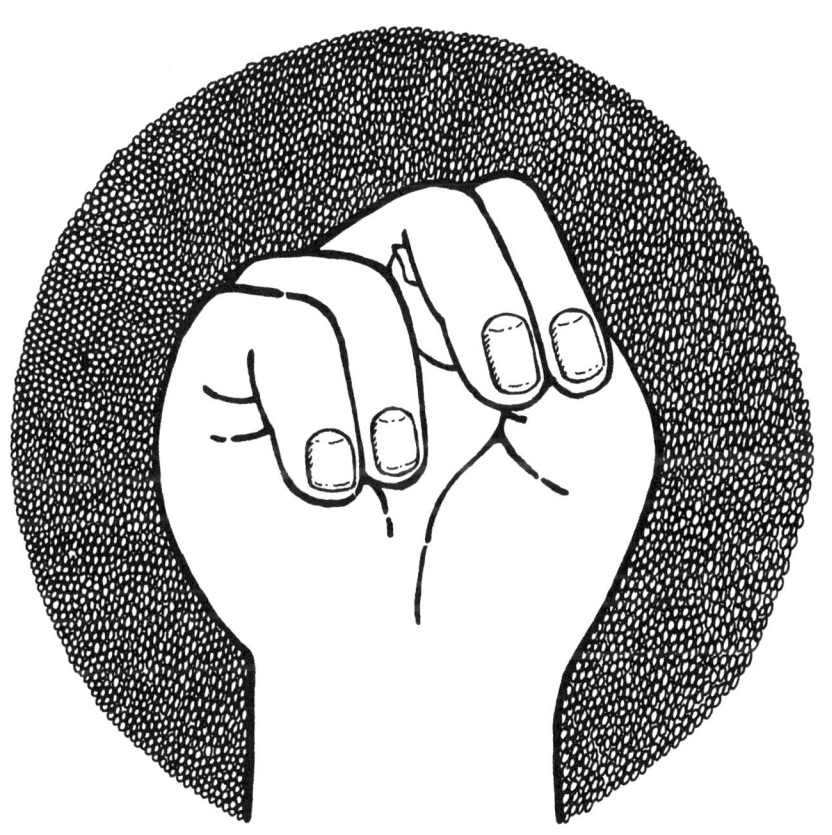

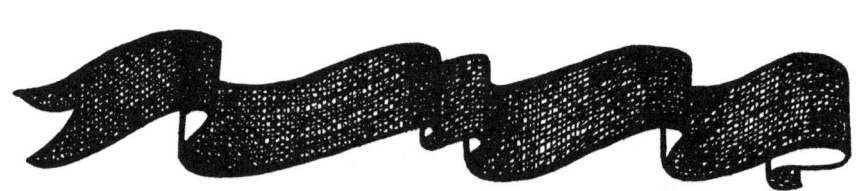

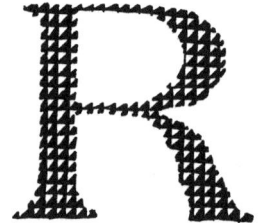

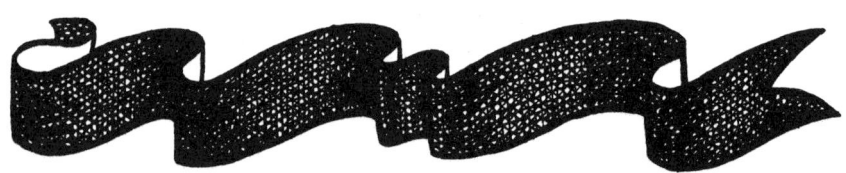

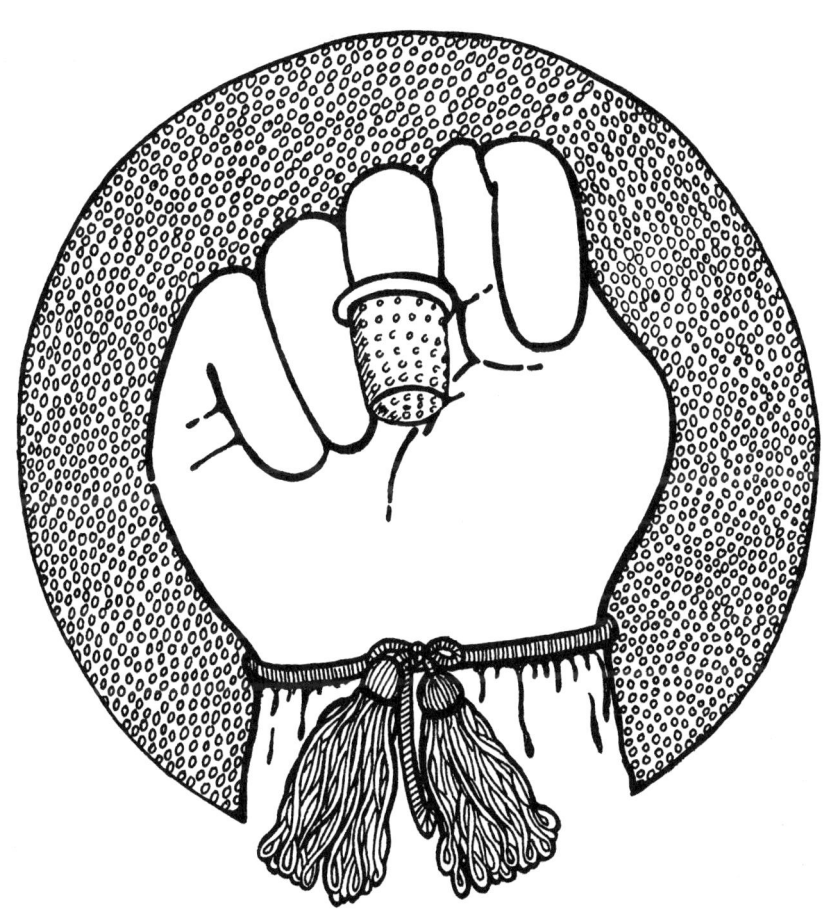

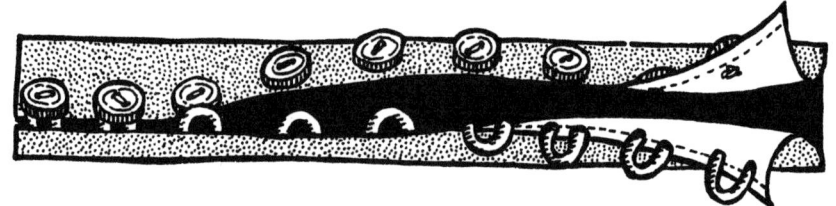

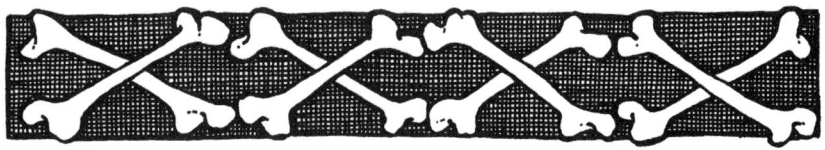

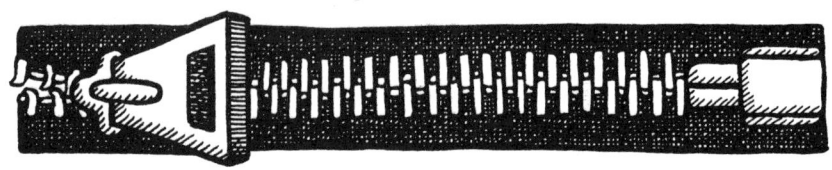

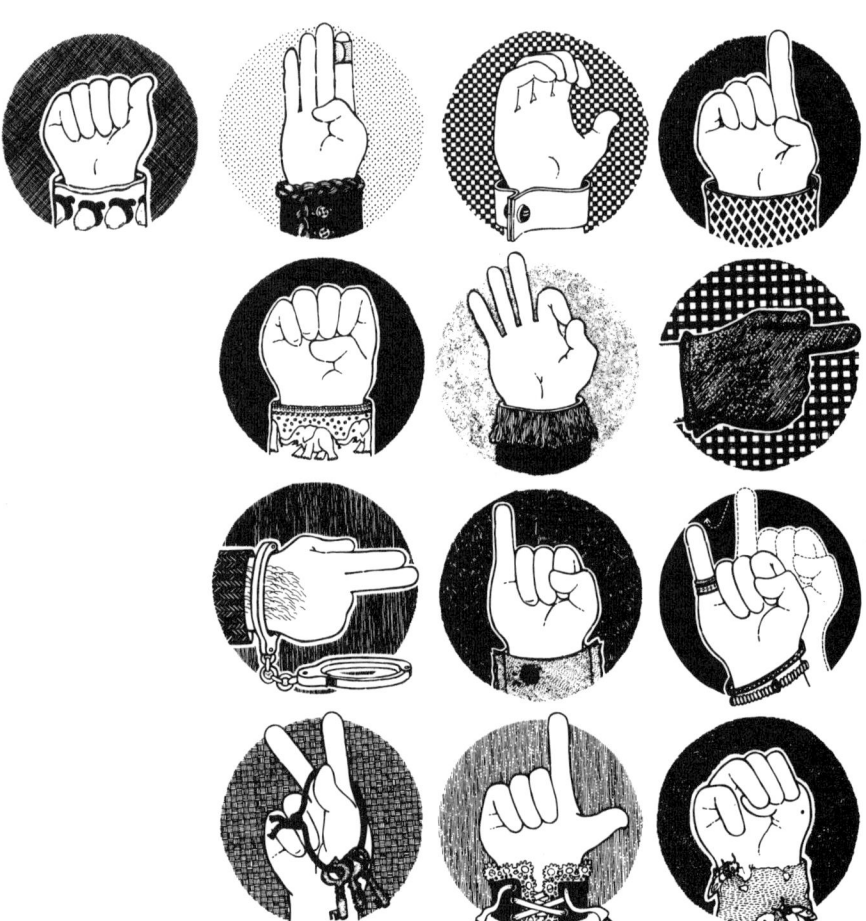

A   Acorn   Applique

B   Buttons Band-Aid Braid Buttonholes

C   Cuff links Checks Cuff

D   Diamonds

E   Embroidery Elephants

F   Fringe Fur

G   Gathering Gingham Glove

H   Herringbone Hooks Hairy Handcuff

I   Inkspots Inside out

J   Jewelry

K   Knots Keys

L   Lace Lacing

M   Moth Moth holes Mole

N Needlepoint Needle Nails
O Ovals Octagons
P Pins Patch Plaid Polka dots
Q Quilt
R Ribbons Rip Ruffle
S Scallops Stitches Stars Stripes Scar
T Tassels Thimble Tie
U Unbuttoned
V Vines Veins
W Weaving Wart Wristwatch Wooly
X X-ray
Y Yarn
Z Zipper Zigzag

Other books you may want to read:

FEELING FREE
by Mary Beth Sullivan, Alan Brightman, Joseph Blatt,

A SHOW OF HANDS
by Mary Beth Sullivan, Linda Bourke

Available from Addison-Wesley Publishing Company, Inc.